PRESENTED TO

_____

FROM

_____

THE
Transparent
Life

30 Proven Ways to Live Your Best

NAOMI
JUDD

NASHVILLE, TENNESSEE
www.jcountryman.com

The Transparent Life
Copyright © 2005 by Naomi Judd

Published by J. Countryman®, a division of Thomas Nelson, Inc.,
Nashville, Tennessee 37214

J. Countryman® is a trademark of Thomas Nelson, Inc.

Unless otherwise indicated, all quotations from the Bible are from
The New King James Version (NKJV) ©1979, 1980, 1982, 1992,
Thomas Nelson, Inc., Publisher. Used by permission. New Century
Version® (NCV). Copyright © 1987, 1988, 1991 by Thomas Nelson,
Inc. All rights reserved. The King James Version of the Bible (KJV).

Design: Koechel Peterson & Associates | Minneapolis, MN
Project Editor: Pat Matuszak
Project Manager: Kathy Baker

ISBN 1 4041 0336 8

Printed and bound in the United States of America

www.thomasnelson.com | www.jcountryman.com

www.naomijudd.com

CHAPTER ONE

CHOICES

the Good, the Bad, and the Ugly

AS YOU SIT THERE READING this page, how happy, peaceful, and fulfilled are you, on a scale of one to ten? Are you outside the door of the life you always thought you should have, desperately banging on it to get in? Do you look forward to your day? Or do you feel like you're stuck in a rut?

The concepts in this book will help you find your own unique path through the issues you're facing and make the choices that will bring greater satisfaction. I want to prove to you that no one's born with their destiny stamped on their forehead. Nobody's born a great anything. We make the choices to fulfill our destiny. Within these book covers are questions that will increase your awareness of the answers that are locked inside you.

PERSONAL QUESTIONS

What's your definition of success? One way to identify your own definition of success is to ask yourself: If I won the lottery, what would I change in my life? What would I keep the same?

HAPPINESS IS . . .

. . . a state of well-being, full of contentment that comes from being satisfied with whatever you have. I'm happiest when I'm aware of my spiritual connection and fully experiencing the present moment.

A NOTE FROM NAOMI

Let me go on the record now and say that there is nothing special about Naomi Judd. I'm not an expert. (Isn't an "expert" really just somebody from out of town with a slideshow and flow-charts?) I am a student of human behavior, a "Road" scholar with a Ph.D. from the School of Hard Knocks. America is my research lab. I hope you will learn more about your potential as I share with you. I'm going to explain how I learned to make the choices that allowed me not only to survive but to thrive—to be happier, healthier, and more content than I have ever been before. I've done it against great odds—and I'm confident you can too.

WISDOM
from the Bible

*"How precious also are
Your thoughts to me, O God!
…Search me, O God,
and know my heart;
Try me, and know
my anxieties…
lead me in the way
everlasting."*
PSALM 139:17-24

I have been delighted to learn that the scriptural roots of my previous book allowed it to be used as a teaching tool in church study groups as well as book club discussion groups. In this new book, each topic will contain key Bible verses to give you new ideas that will guide and strengthen your spirit along with your mind and body.

I'm satisfied that every obstacle I've faced has been part of a much bigger plan. Suffering makes sense if you can step back and view it in a larger context. Everything in your life and mine is exactly the way it's supposed to be. This was a huge revelation for me! Discovering this universal concept lets me breathe a lot easier, gives me greater peace of mind, and allows me to expand instead of contract.

You may know that in 1964, at age eighteen, back in the small town of Ashland, Kentucky, I missed my high school graduation to give birth to Wynonna. Then, in my twenties, I had an unhappy first marriage. It did, however, produce my darling Ashley. The inevitable divorce forced me to become a desperate, single, working mom struggling alone with my two girls. Without skills or an education, I was relegated to minimum–wage jobs and even had to resort to welfare. It was desperate and demeaning. So in my thirties I put myself through college and got an RN degree.

In 1979, I took a giant risk chasing a preposterous dream. I arrived in Nashville in an old, beat-up car with two young, high-spirited girls in the backseat. At age thirty-seven, I turned the fantasy of our becoming recording artists into reality. In my forties and fifties, I've proven medical authorities wrong after they coldly handed me a death sentence of three years because of hepatitis C.

Today I'm radiantly healthy and happier than ever! I'm using my restored energy and life lessons to help you learn about yourself. Folks like you come up to me on the street, in restaurants and airports, or at the grocery counter and ask how I survived. You wonder how my husband, Larry, and I have managed to stay in love. It has been frustrating for me not to have time to respond with answers. I've learned so much about how easy it is to make smarter choices. You, too, can achieve greater peace of mind. That's why I'm excited to have finally written this book for you.

CHAPTER TWO

KNOW *How You Feel*

WHEN I LEARNED I had hepatitis C, I studied everything I could get my hands on about this "silent killer" that will kill four times more Americans than AIDS in the next decade. Bill Moyers's groundbreaking PBS documentary series *Healing and the Mind* launched me into an investigation that wound up saving my life. It encouraged me to search for a different path to healing. I delved into understanding how we are whole beings with emotions, lifestyles, and spiritual needs. I learned how our lifestyles can cause all sorts of mental distress and disease, and that good health is much more than just the absence of disease. I was shocked to discover that 85 percent of all illnesses are related to stress. In fact, the World Health Organization has proclaimed stress to be the number-one global epidemic.

Because I chose to be proactive in fighting my disease, I had a physical break*through* instead of a physical break*down*. I've won a bitter, frightening battle and have been pronounced free of the virus.

Each time we squarely face and successfully handle a problem, we become aware of even more options. In these upcoming pages, you're going to assemble your own personal toolbox of emotional, physical, and spiritual tools. Then you can reach for them anytime you desire to fix something in your mind, body, or spirit.

PERSONAL QUESTIONS

As soon as we give ourselves the power to seek meaning in a challenge, we also give ourselves the power to change. What was your first big milestone, challenge, or crisis? Looking back, what did you learn from that event? What characteristic traits did it bring out in you?

PEACE IS . . .

Just as health isn't simply the absence of disease, peace of mind isn't just the absence of problems. Peace of mind comes from your ability to deal with issues.

A NOTE FROM NAOMI

Peace of mind is the ultimate goal. I've met kings and queens, world leaders, presidents, movie stars, rock stars, and every kind of famous personage. I can tell you we all want the same thing— peace of mind.

WISDOM
from the Bible

"You will keep him in perfect peace, Whose mind is stayed on You, Because he trusts in You."

ISAIAH 26:3

Epiphanies are sudden, intuitive perceptions or insights. I've come to recognize them as symbolic revelations from God. One such moment of truth happened when I realized my life had greater meaning than the choices I'd been making. I began to see that choices are sacred. God created us and gives us the opportunities to make choices. This means we can become co-creators with God in deciding our future. I've come to understand that there is an invisible, spiritual world. As we make inspired conscious choices, we're opening up to infinite possibilities. God is always there—invisible but all-knowing and available for us to turn to.

When it comes time to make a choice, realizing what we *don't* want can help us see what we *do* want to do. My epiphany caused me to look back on my choices with newly informed eyes. I immediately became clear about what I didn't want anymore. I didn't like the way I'd been raising Wy and Ashley, and I no longer wanted any part of the over-stimulated, materialistic, phony Hollywood lifestyle.

What was important to me was Wy and Ash knowing their heritage and being close to our family. I also wanted time and opportunity to tune in to them. Once I became aware of the huge discrepancy between the choices I'd been making and my true values, I began making the necessary steps for bringing my life into alignment with my values.

Peace Prize

Your relationship with yourself predicts the kind of relationships you'll have with others. Get ready for an epiphany as you come to understand how your self-esteem affects everything. The more we understand ourselves and what's standing in the way of our being as happy and healthy as we can, the more eager we become to risk following our dreams and offering our gifts to others; the more worthy we feel, the more we choose peace of mind. When we trust ourselves and the process of becoming, we evolve. Life is a process. We either find a way or make a way, one day at a time. Today is the first day of the rest of an altogether more peaceful and fulfilling life. You can consciously choose a better way of relating to yourself and others.

CHAPTER THREE

HOPE
Helps you Cope

IF YOU'RE HAVING a hard time and are at the end of your rope, here's one thing you can do—tie a knot and hang on! Hope will help you get through. The pain you may be experiencing is certainly real, but it can be temporary. I've learned you can use it as the motivation for your **H**ealing **O**f **P**ainful **E**xperiences (HOPE).

There have been so many scary times when hope was really all I had. Through the years, when I was broke or troubled by relationship problems, hope was the gift I could always give myself to keep from sinking deeper into my fears. Hope was my constant companion during what I call my "dark night of the soul," the time when I was ill with hepatitis C. The last word I spoke onstage every night in each city of my Farewell Tour was "hope." After singing "Love Can Build a Bridge," I left the stage with this self-fulfilling prophecy.

Louise Hay is a superstar in the world of healing. Today she's a best-selling author and speaker, but Louise was sexually abused at age five and subjected to extreme misery and poverty as a child of the Depression. But she was determined to overcome her circumstances. She became an expert on how not to let your past control your future. Louise literally wrote the book, *You Can Heal Your Life*, which I highly recommend. Don't be limited by what happened yesterday.

Can you allow yourself to believe you are more than your past?

COURAGE IS . . .

It takes courage to be proactive and embrace hope instead of being reactive to depression or defeat. As John Wayne put it, "Courage is being afraid but saddling up anyway." Being scared is what comes before courage.

A NOTE FROM NAOMI

I personally can tell you that it takes courage to start making life-altering changes. Some people would rather stay in a bad situation because they haven't evolved enough to find the courage to change. I was scared before I worked up the courage to go back to school in my 30's. But I earned much more than an RN degree in the process. I earned self-respect!

"Where your treasure is,

there your heart will be also."

MATTHEW 6:21

No one in my family had worked in health care. I didn't even know a nurse. Yet I realized I had always been drawn toward helping others. I soon realized that, as it says in Matthew, that was where my heart was. It became clear to me that my children and my desire to alleviate suffering in others were my priorities. Nursing appeared to be the right step.

Evenings I cared for Wy and Ash, but I could waitress after putting them to bed. It was a grueling, hard time—waitressing until 1 A.M., getting up to go to class, taking care of the kids. What kept me going on this path was that I immediately started feeling better. As I opened up to discovering more about myself, mistakes became less frequent.

My pal George Lucas, creator and director of *Star Wars*, shared with me how his own early struggles trying to get funding for his first movies then digging out from their subsequent flops had prepared him for his eventual mega-success. He said, "It's okay to lose; just don't lose the lesson."

When Olympic gold-medal skater Scott Hamilton was asked what the most difficult jump is, I understood his answer: "The one you have to do right after you've fallen." No matter what the circumstances of our lives, we all have the power to reverse them from a curse to a blessing.

CHAPTER FOUR

Know Who You Were
and Who You Are Now

IT'S BAD ENOUGH if somebody hurt you while you were growing up. But if you continue to let the pain mess with you as an adult, you are allowing the abuse to happen all over again. No matter how seriously you have been wronged, it's critical to your future well-being that you deal with your anger and resentment once and for all.

Because I witnessed my mom and dad's acrimonious divorce, I regrettably did some of the same things to Wy and Ashley when I divorced their dad. I hadn't yet forgiven their dad or acknowledged my own responsibility in the failure of the relationship. I didn't realize that every child desperately needs to feel that each parent is good.

But Wynonna chose to break this negative cycle. Her pain from my parents' divorce and my own disastrous handling of my divorce caused her consciously to choose not to pass on our mistakes. She took the high road by not letting her divorce interfere with her children's perceptions of their dad. She broke a harmful family tradition. She reversed the curse of divorce by practicing forgiveness.

Do you have bad memories that haunt you? Do you use any kind of "emotional aspirin" to cope with them?

HEART KNOWLEDGE IS . . .

. . . being genuinely tuned in to your feelings so you can consciously begin to choose what to let go.

A NOTE FROM NAOMI

People I know personally who've lost weight, gone through rehab, or ditched a bad relationship say their breakthroughs happened after they finally realized that their behavior had been rooted in an attempt to feed some emotional or spiritual emptiness.

Jesus saw him lying there,
and knew that he already had been
in that condition a long time.
He said to him,
"Do you want to be made well?"

JOHN 5:6

Jesus knew that the man lying beside the healing pool at Bethesda had come there hoping to be made well. But He asked the man to speak his desire aloud for all to hear.

One of the most interesting people I came across during my foray into the ways people heal was an expert on why some folks can't seem to discover what's standing in their way. Carolyn Myers spent some time explaining to me how some people actually identify with their physical illness or emotional suffering. They become stuck as "wound addicts."

Did you ever consider that you may be using your disease or emotional wound as an excuse—an excuse to feel important, avoid honest communication, or cover up some failure? Rather than doing the work of discovering what's standing in your way, could you be getting even more attached to being broken or sick?

While I was ill the time came to renew my car registrations. I spontaneously chose personalized plates for our cars. The words FAITH and HOPE immediately came to mind because aiming for a positive outcome is the way my mind works. It's always in the forefront of my thinking. As Samuel Johnson said, "Hope is itself a species of happiness, and perhaps the chief happiness which this world affords."

Only by understanding what's standing in our way can we enable true healing and happiness to take place. We deserve to move beyond old wounds. The promise of Christ makes all things new.

OPTIMISM

is the faith

that leads to achievement.

Nothing can be done

without *hope* and *confidence*.

HELEN KELLER

May our Lord Jesus Christ himself

and God our Father encourage you

and strengthen you in every

good thing you do and say.

God loved us, and through his grace

he gave us a good hope

and encouragement

that continues forever.

2 THESSALONIANS 2:16 NCV

CHAPTER FIVE

You Be THE JUDGE

WHAT HAPPENS TO US doesn't matter as much as what we do with it. Despite the pain I felt over my parents' divorce, I used what I was witnessing and feeling to positive effect. I decided to become my own judge and jury as I investigated my own case. Until that point in my life, my own choices hadn't been serving me too well. I began to uncover clues to the similarities between my parents' challenges and my own. I dissected my parents' individual strengths and weaknesses. As a result, I began to see how my personality had been influenced by them. Doing this detective work was the only way to get a grip on how early influences were still playing out in my daily choices. Once I became aware of these influences, I could see how to figure out some different choices.

The beliefs you and I hold today are the result of our own unique memories and experiences, which began developing from the moment we were born. Each one of us is as totally original as a snowflake or a fingerprint.

PERSONAL QUESTIONS

Have you ever mentally looked at your parents as strangers and objectively analyzed how they were raised? Consider exploring it with living relatives and recording them as they talk about their memories of growing up. Ask family members to share the meaning of their mementoes.

THE GREATEST FAMILY GIFT IS . . .

. . . creating a place where we grow both roots and wings.

A NOTE FROM NAOMI

I remember my mom standing over me when I was a little girl, teaching, "Daughter of mine, you can do anything if you just set your mind to it" and "Judd women always land on their own two feet." Mama also instructed me never to let anybody tell me who I am. She always encouraged us four kids to live our own lives. ✎

To thine own self be true.

WILLIAM SHAKESPEARE

"Behold, You desire truth
in the inward parts,
And in the hidden part
You will make me
to know wisdom."

PSALM 51:6

How we were raised is instrumental in determining whether we are now comfortable with our feelings and the emotional reactions we tend to have. We are products of both heredity (nature) and environment (nurture).

Looking at ourselves in a mirror is analogous to looking at an iceberg. We see only the tip. That's the product of our heredity, which determines our physical appearance. Most of the iceberg is hidden under the fathoms of the sea. So it is with our emotions as well.

If someone in our family had depression or anxiety, we may also be genetically vulnerable (nature). We also may be susceptible to depression if we were raised in a depressing or anxiety-provoking environment (nurture). Having a genetic link and/or an unhealthy home environment increases our need to be aware of how our emotions drive bad habits. This makes a difference. We now can choose to modify our behavior. This awareness of family medical history becomes the source of our power to change the course of our future. We are self-determined instead of being driven by nature or our past.

Every time you study your features in a mirror (probably looking for faults), keep excavating to uncover your feelings. This is important, so ask yourself questions about whether you feel safe in your most important relationships. Whom do you trust the most? What's frustrating in your daily life? Look back on your day and think about feelings that sprang up. As you unearth and face these feelings, potent emotional reactions will start to tumble out.

Anytime you start to feel uncomfortable, you'll know you've hit a nerve. So stop. Stay with that emotion for a minute. Let it wash over you. It offers valuable information. Ask out loud to the mirror, "What's going on?" Getting straight with yourself is a crucial step to self-discovery.

CHAPTER SIX

HEAL
with the Power of Love

WHEN MY GIRLFRIEND Reba McEntire showed me around her home one night after supper, she proudly pointed out a picture of her dad, Clark. I knew that he'd come out of the rodeo circuit in their small town in Oklahoma. Reba smiled as she began to explain how art imitates life. Her number-one country single at the time was "The Greatest Man I Never Knew." She related how her father had been one of those typically hardworking, but unaffectionate, distant fathers. But he'd recently undergone surgery and, on the way into the operating room, had surprised her by saying, "I love you."

Guys like our fathers were strong and silent in those days. Daddy loved me very much, but he never knew how to return my ebullient emotions. He worked like a brute over at the gas station so that I could have a good home, plenty of food, piano lessons, and even braces on my teeth. In those days that was typical of how men showed love for their families.

Growing up, Reba and I both craved more affection and expression, so we've compensated as adults by becoming professional communicators.

What was important in your childhood home? Beliefs are based on memories and experiencies. Values are what's important to you. Think of two ways your family shaped your beliefs and values.

TRANSFORMATION IS . . .

I love the word "transformation." **Trans** means "above," "across." **Form** refers to your limits, shapes, or boundaries. The suffix—**ion** means "the experience of." When we experience a transformation, a changing of the shape we're in, we can have the experience of rising above our previous limits.

A NOTE FROM NAOMI

The first prophetic entry my Mom made into my baby book was, "She has a vivid imagination." Daddy's strong work ethic also made an indelible impression on me. He'd say, "Be the labor great or small, do it well or not at all."

Above all things

have fervent love for one another,

for "love will cover a multitude of sins."

1 PETER 4:8

My Judd grandparents, aunts, and uncles lived on a remote farm in rural Louisa, Kentucky. They would put me up on the kitchen table at their farmhouse, where I would dance and sing my heart out. They'd whistle, cheer, and stomp their feet. I see now how this really boosted my self-esteem.

Decades later, I would find myself performing in concert halls around the world, singing and dancing just as I had when I was a little girl. My family's love and encouragement helped me think of myself in that winner category by the time I was three years old.

Based on early experiences, we feel like either winners or losers; we're blessed with a healthy self-concept or cursed with low self-esteem. If you had good experiences with your parents as a child, you'll be more apt today to respond favorably to authority figures like teachers, firemen, policemen, and bosses. You might even have become one. On the other hand, if your parents physically abused or neglected you, your perception of authority is probably skewed. You may be rebellious and have trouble following rules.

As adults, the more we become aware of what happened to us as children, the more we can choose to separate from early imprinting that doesn't serve us. Finding out what took place in our formative years is the first step in discovering how we've become the eay we are now. The more we understand what our unique childhood tracks were, the more we can consciously choose whether we want to be on that particular train anymore.

CHAPTER SEVEN

EXAMINING
Memories Through Adult Eyes

YOU COULDN'T CHOOSE the family you were born into, but now you're older and you're reading this book! You see the world with adult eyes. Just as you've outgrown the clothes you wore as a child, you've now evolved to a greater capacity for understanding behavior.

No matter what happened to us as children, as adults we must take responsibility for the choices we are making now. Psychologists say that after age thirty, we no longer can blame our parents for failures and problems. That's because, although we can't change what happened to us as children, we can revisit the past, view it though informed adult eyes, take the lessons, and begin making conscious new choices based on our evolved understanding. We're free to become what we've wanted.

PERSONAL QUESTION

Think back. Who and what influenced who you are and what you believe about yourself?

EMOTIONAL CLIMATE IS . . .

. . . the atmosphere that surrounds you in your environment where you are right now. Is it peaceful and encouraging or angry and discouraging? Emotionally we inhale that climate. We either are nourished by it if it is positive and appropriate or suffocated by it if it is hostile and chaotic.

> ### A NOTE FROM NAOMI
> *When you assess your early memories, think also about your extended family, including grandparents, aunts, uncles, and cousins. You can learn a lot about your childhood by looking at your baby pictures, home movies, or baby books. Were you in clean clothes? Were you smiling? Were there toys, pets, and friends?*

Surely goodness and mercy
will follow me all the days of my life;
And I will dwell in the house
of the LORD forever.

PSALM 23:6

It's fascinating to discover how you've developed your likes and dislikes, even what kind of environment you're drawn to live in. You might not recognize it, but every day your childhood is still influencing your life!

Our families shaped our beliefs through our first and formative experiences. For instance, my daddy passed on his ethic of hard work; Mom, her belief in the importance of family and traditions.

Think back to how your childhood home was furnished and kept. What activities did your family make sure to take time for? Who did they include in their circle of friends? How did they listen to you or fail to listen when you spoke?

All parents want their children to have better lives than they did. It's a tribute to our parents that we not only carry on their good traits but also learn from their shortcomings. We do it not only for ourselves, but for those who will come after us. Don't let your heir down!

CHAPTER EIGHT

EVERYONE
Has Their Own Reality

THE MORE WE SHED LIGHT on our past, the more we're able to see that we should make conscious choices to create healthier behavior. It's all about examining our emotions, because they define our behaviorial lives.

Can you guess, besides parental influence, how your personality was formed? Birth order!

Parents have high expectations for their firstborn children, and they are raised to lead and set an example for younger children. Siblings go out of their way to be different from one another, so second-born children start trying to contrast early. They're going to be different because they want to be separate and autonomous. The youngest child in the family holds a special position as "the baby" of the family and never gets dethroned.

Could you be falsely believing there is something either lacking or superior about yourself, when it's purely a manifestation of birth-order?

Do you have ongoing, current, adult relationships with your siblings? Or is it possible that you still have frozen mental snapshots of them as kids?

PSYCHOLOGICAL BIRTH ORDER IS . . .

. . . when major events or time lapses between children cause exceptions to the usual birth order generalizations. Family crises (such as when a child is born after another one dies) or long gaps between the birth of children may result in children having "only child" personalities even if they are in a big family.

A NOTE FROM NAOMI

An experience when my sister and I were single working moms sharing a house led to my awareness of birth-order differences. As I listened to Margaret describing her experiences growing up, I learned more about her and adjusted some opinions. It was clear that despite our having the same genetic parents and being raised under the same roof, we were distinctly different individuals. We formed different realities about many beliefs. Yet today we're best friends because we understand how we got over our separate realities.

Bear one another's burdens
and so fulfill the law of Christ.

GALATIANS 6:2

It's natural to expect our blood relatives to think and act just like us. But they don't, and you'd better wrap your mind around that! Sometimes the differences are rooted in birth order. This is a BASIC concept every family needs to grasp. If four people witness a car wreck, you'll get four different versions of what happened. The same is true for family life.

Often, as adults we have trouble viewing our brothers and sisters as contemporaries. After we move into our own homes and create our own families, we tend to lose touch. We carry around frozen mental snapshots of our siblings—the bossy girl, the funny boy, the quiet one, the smart one—and this stands in the way of our seeing who they are now. Consider how your separate realities are keeping you from seeing your brother or sister as they've evolved into adults.

Once we see how important timing and early sibling interactions were in drafting the blueprints of our personalities, we can begin correcting and updating those blueprints. This can help us put our early hurts into perspective and can help us heal. Or this exploration can illuminate destructive patterns we've been carrying with us into the present. Another great hope of this process is drawing closer to those who shared our childhood with us. A loving family is one of life's greatest rewards.

CHAPTER NINE

FORGIVENESS
Is Emotional Housecleaning

NEWS FLASH! Forgiveness is not for the person who offended you. It is for you. In order for me to even think about forgiving, I needed solid reasons.

Forgiveness doesn't mean you have to deny what happened. You certainly don't have to condone or forget the wrong! Rather, forgiveness is choosing to stop your vengeance from diminishing you by continuing to drag you down to someone else's level.

Evil is very real. That makes forgiveness very tricky. But by forgiving, we overcome evil with our goodwill.

The people who hurt you were troubled and in great pain themselves. You might have been a victim of a victim. But let the cycle stop there—forgive.

PERSONAL QUESTION

Is the emotional scar tissue of anger and resentment causing you to disconnect from yourself and others?

RESENTMENT IS . . .

. . . a second-hand emotion, a cover for underlying feelings that have never been expressed. That's why you need to assess what damage was done to you by the person you want to forgive. Then create a boundary that will help you protect yourself. This boundary might be something like, "I will leave the room if someone is verbally abusing me."

A NOTE FROM NAOMI

Forgiveness is the quicker picker-upper. Once we've 'fessed up to a misdeed and made amends, it's time to take off the handcuffs and turn ourselves loose! As we allow forgiveness to free us, we begin to really celebrate the best our lives can offer. ✎

*"If you forgive men
their trespasses,
your heavenly Father
will also forgive you."*

MATTHEW 6:14

I don't know about you, but I need to be forgiven. Jesus Christ died publicly, nailed to a wooden cross, sacrificing Himself by asking God the Father to forgive the sins of all of us. Heaven forgave His crucifiers: *"Father, forgive them, for they do not know what they do"* (Luke 23:34). Kind of makes our reluctance to forgive seem pretty stinkin' petty, doesn't it? Jesus is my mentor, and I strive to live out the practical lessons He taught.

Often, in our anger toward another, we come to realize that the person we most need to forgive is ourselves. I was much harder mentally on myself than on anyone else. If this is true for you as well, try Joan Borysenko's steps toward self-forgiveness:

1. Recognize what you're responsible for and holding on to.
2. Confess your story to another person and to God.

3. Consider what specific action needs to be taken to resolve things with the other person.
4. Reflect on what you have learned. Self-forgiveness opens up opportunities for growth.
5. Realize that anger is biologically toxic and can make you ill.
6. Continually look to God for help.

Bless the LORD, O my soul,
And forget not all His benefits:
Who forgives all your iniquities,
Who heals all your diseases,
Who redeems your life from destruction,
Who crowns you with lovingkindness and tender mercies,
Who satisfies your mouth with good things,
So your youth is renewed like the eagle's.
The LORD executes righteousness
And justice for all who are oppressed.
. . . The LORD is merciful and gracious,
Slow to anger, and abounding in mercy.
. . . He has not dealt with us according to our sins,
Nor punished us according to our iniquities.

PSALM 103:2-6, 8, 10

*The weak
can never forgive.
Forgiveness
is the attribute
of the strong.*

MOHANDAS GHANDI

FOREGIVENESS
is the giving,

and so the receiving, of life.

GEORGE MacDONALD

Forgiveness is a funny thing. It warms the heart and cools the sting.

WILLIAM A. WARD

There is no revenge so complete as forgiveness.

JOSH BILLINGS

God has chosen you
and made you his holy people.
He loves you. So always do these things:
Show mercy to others, be kind, humble,
gentle, and patient.
Get along with each other, and forgive each other.
If someone does wrong to you, forgive that person
because the Lord forgave you. Do all these things;
but most important, love each other.
Love is what holds you all together in perfect unity.
Let the peace that Christ gives control
your thinking, because you were all called
together in one body to have peace.
Always be thankful.

COLOSSIANS 3:12-15 NCV

CHAPTER TEN

IS YOUR WORK
Working for You?

TOMMY WALLER is a jovial farmer who sells his organic vegetables and his wife Sherri's homemade jams, jellies, and baked goods in front of a small grocery store in our village. One hot afternoon while chatting as he was weighing some fresh-picked tomatoes, I learned about Tommy's previous life. He had been an officer with Federal Express. He and his wife had been part of the briefcases, nice-cars, and big-home set— until one day they had a breakthrough and realized they were not living their passion. Their passion was family, connecting with nature, and a simpler, more rewarding daily life. They now live contentedly on a farm with their seven children, with no TV, telephone, fax, email, or computer. They practice voluntary simplicity so they can live a more satisfying life.

Job dissatisfaction has been found to be a better predictor of heart attack and disease than high blood pressure, obesity, or even smoking. When you follow your passions, you preserve or enhance your physical and mental well-being. Are you dying to make a living?

What are you drawn to? What makes your heart sing?

NAME YOUR BRAIN

Right-brain talents are creative, expressive, and musical. Left-brain talents are rational, mathematical, and logical.

A NOTE FROM NAOMI

What are your passions? A sure sign of passion is the degree of satisfaction an activity provides. Another indicator is losing track of time when you are doing something particular. Make a list of everything you love to do and add to the list every time you discover you're enjoying yourself.

Commit your works to the LORD,

And your thoughts will be established.

PROVERBS 16:3

Once you identify your strengths and passions, you've got to build your life around them every way you can! Don't try to correct your weaknesses any longer. It's time to shift your focus from struggling with your weak areas to relishing and building up your strong areas. When you identify what you love and are good at, you're equipped with powerful self-knowledge to help you advance along your path.

Research shows that each of us has five core strengths. These are talents you can't learn in school, by watching someone else, or through a book. They come from self-awareness. That's not to say you have to be perfect at every facet of something for it to be a strength. It does mean that you should focus on figuring out what your strengths are.

CHAPTER ELEVEN

PAY
ATTENTION
to Your Personal Radar

INTUITION IS OUR INNER KNOWING, the part of us that serves as an inner compass. Think of it as a North Star to guide each of us to our destiny. It is one of the most powerful, most underused resources at our disposal. It's our inner wisdom and—if callibrated to God's standards—is always going to steer us right. It's our one trustworthy source of knowledge and has our best interests at heart.

The value of this "language" created by our brain and bodies allows us to gain perception, insight, understanding, and compassion about our past and to make decisions about the future. Intuition can assist us emotionally, physically, and spiritually. It can help us decide if a person, job, move, or treatment is right for us, despite what anyone else is saying.

Do you ever feel that you have to ignore your inner voice to please others or because they wouldn't accept your real feelings about things?

INTUITION IS . . .

. . . our sixth sense. It allows us to perceive or sense outside the range of our usual five senses (vision, hearing, smell, taste, body sensations) to greatly widen our doors of knowing. It uses the body to send messages of well-being, foreboding, pain, or disease.

> A NOTE FROM NAOMI
> *My friend Dr. Judith Orloff (a psychiatrist at UCLA) calls me an "empathic intuitive," meaning that I sense other people's problems. I sense them viscerally and pick up visual clues as well as how and what they are about to say. I try to use my God-given ability to stimulate intuitive gifts within others.*

WISDOM
from the Bible

*An angel of the Lord
appeared to Joseph
in a dream, saying,
"Arise, take the young
Child and His mother,
flee to Egypt,
and stay there until I
bring you word;
for Herod will seek
the young Child
to destroy Him."*

MATTHEW 2:13

Pay attention to powerful, vivid, and recurring dreams as well as the whispers of intuition during the day. Carl Jung believed "dreams are a little hidden door into the innermost and most secret messages of the soul."

My girlfriend Judith believes "the future of medicine lies in reincorporating intuition and spirituality—vital parts of our wisdom usually disenfranchised from health care. With intuitive healing, every aspect of one's being gains a vote in the search for well-being, opening the door to total health—of our bodies, our emotions, and our sexuality."

Now when Herod was dead, behold,
an angel of the Lord appeared in a dream
to Joseph in Egypt, saying, "Arise, take the young
Child and His mother, and go
to the land of Israel, for those who sought the young
Child's life are dead."

MATTHEW 2:19-20

Begin Every Day
with Solitude and Self-Assurance

HOW MANY TIMES A DAY do you groan, "All I want is a little peace and quiet"? That's your wise, caring intuition telling you that it can't get through unless you give yourself silence and solitude as part of your everyday routine.

Those important messages from our intuition can't get through unless we stop long enough to listen. Being alone helps me keep my sanity and allows me to be centered, so I decided to consciously make room for solitude wherever I was. I can't live without it.

Solitude first allows me to empty my mind of all the needless worry about others' needs. Then slowly but consciously it lets me fill up that space with my inner knowing. Today's culture is obsessed with doing, busyness, and producing. It shows little value for allowing us to just be who we are— a human *being* instead of a human *doing*.

PERSONAL QUESTION

Do you struggle with a persistent feeling that you should be busy all the time? Starting tomorrow morning, choose to take twenty minutes to be silent within before you go out into the noisy world.

SOLITUDE IS . . .

. . . the absence of human activity. Solitude is refreshment for your soul that allows time for the small voice of your inner knowing to be heard.

A NOTE FROM NAOMI

When I start my morning with solitude, I enjoy the day so much more. Plus, I'm then able to give others my best. I give out of my overflow. I would no more pass up my solitude time than I would leave my house hungry. I call it my "zoneola."

It is good to give thanks to the LORD,
And to sing praises to Your name,
  O Most High;
To declare Your lovingkindness in the morning,
  And Your faithfulness every night.

PSALM 92:1-2

Soren Kierkegaard wrote: "I found I had less and less to say, until finally, I became silent, and began to listen. I discovered in the silence the voice of God."

Solitude is creativity's best friend. This is when my best ideas come to me. I settle in my picture-window kitchen with its view of nature. In a spot that's visible from my table, I've planted colorful flowers to attract butterflies and placed bird feeders for hummingbirds and yellow finches. In good weather, I open the windows to the sounds of nature. I inhale deep breaths, relax, and luxuriate in this atmosphere of serenity.

You, too, can create your own unique setting where you can be peacefully alone.

CHAPTER THIRTEEN

GO FOR
Life's Adventure

MAYBE YOU'VE HEARD THE SAYING that life gives us the test first and the lessons later. By the time I was going through nursing school in my mid-thirties, I'd survived lots of tough tests and learned many lessons. To get to this point on my path, I'd taken some risks. But to really be all I could be, I would have to take even more. There was no turning back. I had to embrace risk, knowing deep in my bones that risk allows us to become who we were meant to be.

Risk-taking is a funny thing. Each time you risk, it becomes easier to do. That's because each time you go for it, it further reinforces your self-esteem and offers concrete evidence that you can indeed succeed.

What would you attempt if you knew you couldn't fail?

. . . to be slowly born.

ANTOINE De SAINT-EXUPERY

A NOTE FROM NAOMI

It had been a humungous risk to move my daughters from Hollywood to Appalachia, away from their friends to a remote mountain-top without a TV or telephone. But because I'd chosen to take this risk, we were all three soon to discover who we were meant to be. One languid night, searching for some way to pass the time, I handed 12-year-old Wynonna a cheap plastic guitar someone had given me. There was an immediate flash of recognition, as if she had been reunited with some hidden part of herself. It was a "God wink!" Eight-year-old Ashley discovered books, and her imagination soared. Now she uses that imagination in her career as an actress. ✑

Let us hold fast the confession
of our hope without wavering,
for He who promised is faithful.
And let us consider one another
in order to stir up love and good works.

HEBREWS 10:23-24

Wynonna and I were like two souls longing to fuse but afraid to touch. At a time when our mother-daughter relationship had deteriorated to a chronically combative level, music became the glue holding us together. Singing allowed us to connect in a non-threatening manner and encourage each other's gifts. We felt cautiously hopeful as we began to build something brand new together. Harmony was the literal and figurative result.

For me personally, there was a glorious relief as a mother. *Eureka! Wy's found it! She's going to be okay!* And I was bitten by the music bug, too. My intuition began alerting me that I could use music to fulfill my own passions, which are to connect with and help others, most of all my own child. I knew singing was Wy's destiny, and my responsibility and desire were to support her. Plus, I loved singing with her. It was obviously a passion because it came naturally and I lost track of time. I began writing songs, which became an outlet for the creativity that I'd never known I had. Until then, my life as a single, stuggling mother had been all about grunt work and struggling to survive. Passion allows you to be who you're meant to be.

YOU CAN GET
What You Want

People may make plans in their minds,
but only the LORD can make them come true.
You may believe you are doing right,
but the LORD will judge your reasons.
Depend on the LORD in whatever you do,
and your plans will succeed.

PROVERBS 16:1-3 NCV

We fail more often by timidity than by over-daring.

DAVID GRAYSON

WELL DONE
IS BETTER THAN WELL SAID.

BENJAMIN FRANKLIN

Great minds have purposes, others have wishes.

WASHINGTON IRVING

*"I know what I am planning for you,"
says the LORD.
"I have good plans for you,
not plans to hurt you.
I will give you hope and a good future.
Then you will call my name.
You will come to me and pray to me,
and I will listen to you.
You will search for me.
And when you search for me
with all your heart,
you will find me"*

JEREMIAH 29:11-13 NCV

CHAPTER FOURTEEN

BECOME
Who You Want To Be

A FAN WHO'D BOARDED our tour bus after a concert once asked how we could go onto a stage under a spotlight and sing our hearts out in front of ten thousand strangers every night, and he wondered how Ash could perform in front of a camera. I answered him that loving what we do makes it possible to go ahead and do it. When I asked him what he did, the man had a dead-eyed response. In a monotone, he recited his occupation like a label he'd been branded with. It was clear that he was living a life void of passion and risks.

That's tragic because when you and I don't know our heart's desire, it's meaningless to take a risk. We need to be risking toward something—a dream, a goal, the fulfillment of some heart's desire. When we know ourselves better, we're souped up enough to take chances. We need to visualize the rewards and get excited about them.

Is someone in your life discouraging you from being all that you can be? Could it be a case of the bland leading the bland?

FOLLOWING YOUR DREAM MEANS . . .

. . . taking a risk that allows you to grow. Investing faith in God, in yourself, and in your ability to make your dreams come true.

A NOTE FROM NAOMI

If you believe in God, then believe Him when He says "Beloved, I pray that you may prosper in all things and be in health, just as your soul prospers" (3 JOHN 2 KJV). *Take God up on His promise!*

Looking unto Jesus,
the author and finisher of our faith,
who for the joy that was set before Him
endured the cross, despising the shame,
and has sat down at the right hand
of the throne of God.

HEBREWS 12:2

For we walk by faith, not by sight.

2 CORINTHIANS 5:7

Theodore Roosevelt said, "Far better it is to dare mighty things to win glorious triumphs even though checkered with defeat than to rank with those poor spirits that neither enjoy much nor suffer much because they live in that gray twilight that knows not victory nor defeat."

Researchers in psychology have proven that risk-takers who follow their dreams are happier, more productive, and live longer. Risk attracts other colorful people to you, keeps you moving forward toward your goals, and allows you to grow.

Don't get stuck in a comfort zone. If you put a frog in a pot of water and slowly turn up the heat, the frog will remain in the pot and boil to death. However, if you drop the frog into a pot that's already boiling, it immediately will leap out! Consider for a moment that your present comfort zone is like that steadily heating pot. Get out now! Consider W. C. Fields's admonition: "The only difference between a rut and a grave is the dimensions." Could it be you're living in that "gray twilight" zone?

CHAPTER FIFTEEN

CULTIVATE
Your Love Life Inside and Out

BEHAVIORAL SCIENTISTS say you'll never let yourself have more health, happiness, or success than you feel you deserve. Wow! This means that right this minute you're attracting what you feel worthy of having. Chew on that awhile! So the common denominator for getting all the good stuff in life—health, wealth, good relationships, and even longevity—is self-esteem.

Self-esteem fluctuates over time. You and I are constantly measuring ourselves against our past successes and achievements. If there's a discrepancy between what we've already done and what we still want to do, or if we don't continue to achieve our goals, then our self-esteem may falter. Happily, if we learn to talk lovingly to ourselves and surround ourselves with people who truly love and support us, their words and acts of encouragement eventually will sink into our brains and boost our self-esteem.

PERSONAL QUESTIONS

What's the number-one indicator for how long you're going to live and how happy and successful you'll be? Self-esteem. What would you say your current self-worth score is on a scale of one to ten? What things could you do to increase that score?

SELF-ESTEEM IS . . .

. . . a measurement of how well you feel about yourself, how confident and capable you judge yourself. This includes how attractive you think you are.

A NOTE FROM NAOMI
Friends are like elevators. They either take us up or bring us down. But before we can expect to find love from anyone else, we first have to find it within ourselves. God loves us and wants us to have self-worth and self-respect. ✏

WISDOM FROM THE BIBLE

Two are better than one,

Because they have a good reward

for their labor.

For if they fall, one will lift up his companion.

But woe to him who is alone when he falls,

For he has no one to help him up.

ECCLESIASTES 4:9-10

People who possess an inner core of self-esteem become the masters of their own fates. This is what you and I want. We must choose not to see ourselves as victims of our circumstances. We need to be in charge of our behavior. We can't allow ourselves to be at the mercy of those around us. If we don't feel we are worthy, we won't take responsibility for our lives. We will be stuck in a cycle of feeling out of control and then blame others, which results in further low self-esteem.

We can break the cycle by seeing ourselves as masters of our own fates. By the actions we take and every choice we make, we control, to a great degree, what happens to us. We certainly can control our reactions. As we work on creating high self-esteem we'll soon get more of what we want in life.

Ever hear that country song "Lookin' for Love in All the Wrong Places"? Before you and I can expect to find love with anyone else, we first have to find it within ourselves. Your relationship with yourself is the most basic and crucial one. Who you choose to fall in love with is literally a reflection of how much you love or do not love yourself. Conflict with your partner comes down to a reflection of some conflict going on within yourself. Take a long, hard look at everyone around you; the way they treat you is how you've trained them to treat you.

CHAPTER SIXTEEN

BELIEVE IT
and Receive It

WORDS HOLD THE POWER to get what you want and to help you let go of what you don't want. They act like a lever for taking hold of your mind-body. Words become the verbal manifestation of whatever's going on inside your head. They reflect your inner world to your outer world. Sticks and stones can break your bones, and words can break your heart.

Once you have brought a thought to life by speaking it aloud, it's like an arrow released from a bow. Remember, too, that once your words have left your tongue, they can never come back. A closed mouth gathers no foot. Your words have power to build you up or tear you down emotionally, mentally, and physically. Think twice before you speak. You'll be surprised how holding your tongue can foster self-respect and impress others.

Rather than saying to yourself "I'm special," do you say to yourself, "I don't matter," "She's so much more clever," "I can't hold my own in an argument," or "I can't face their disapproval"?

WORDS ARE . . .

My mother says, "Words are the clothes our thoughts wear." The truth is always in fashion. No wonder the tabloids are called "rags."

A NOTE FROM NAOMI

The most powerful words in the English language are the ones you choose to say to yourself. Our internal dialogue has profound effects on our potential to achieve happiness and success. I meet many people who came from horrible beginnings who've learned how to talk themselves into successful living. If we choose to focus on what's possible and talk to ourselves about what success will look and feel like, good things follow.

WISDOM
from the Bible

Whatever things are true,
whatever things are noble,
whatever things are just,
whatever things are pure,
whatever things are lovely,
whatever things are
of good report,
if there is any virtue
and if there is anything
praiseworthy—
meditate on these things.

PHILIPPIANS 4:8

You and I have beliefs about everything; our weight, appearance, relationships, intelligence, eating habits, work, parenting skills, and how much money we make. Every negative pattern we're engaged in is a result of our own self-limiting beliefs and negative self-talk. We have subtle ways of talking negatively to ourselves. Researchers say that 75 percent of our self-conversations are negative. People who engage in negative self-talk drag their spirits and immune systems down. They harm spirit, mind, and body.

Positive changes can't occur if we think things like the following:

Just my luck.

I never know what to say.

I don't know.

I don't have enough talent.

That's impossible.

I'm so stupid.

I'm too old.

I can't stop smoking.

I never have enough time.

Negative self-talk is verbal self abuse! But right this minute you can change the way you're thinking and talking about your life. Your beliefs are the results of your experiences and memories. Once you tell yourself you're going to have a better experience, your attitude shifts accordingly. You're reading this book because you want to actually begin attracting better experiences.

CHAPTER SEVENTEEN

Say 'Good Morning'
TO GOD!

MENTAL OUTLOOK is more reliable in gauging longevity than cancer, diabetes, high blood pressure, or even heart disease, according to a Rutgers University investigation. The researchers also concluded that a woman who considers herself to be in good health is likely to live longer than another woman who may be in similar physical shape but who considers herself to be in poor health. Begin adding life to your years by adding positive thoughts and words.

Creating positive expectations is a habit you can start developing right now, much in the same way you choose to improve your situation through an exercise routine or diet. As soon as I begin to wake up every morning, I say, "Good morning, God." Some people groan, "Ugh, good God, it's morning!" But there is no wrong side of the bed to get up on—it's all in your head!

PERSONAL QUESTIONS

Keep things in perspective by asking yourself:

"Does this glitch really matter in the overall scheme?

Will I even remember it a year from now?"

REFRAMING IS . . .

A person with positive expectations naturally counts

on something great happening. Psychologists call this

"reframing."

A NOTE FROM NAOMI

Most successful people are creative optimists. Babe Ruth, one of the world's greatest baseball players, struck out 1,330 times. Basketball star Michael Jordan was cut from his high school basketball team. Both continued to talk positively to themselves despite their failures— and look what happened!

Jesus said, "These things I have spoken to you, that in Me you may have peace. In the world you will have tribulation; but be of good cheer, I have overcome the world."

JOHN 16:33

In the Book of 1 Samuel, the Israelite army freaked out when they saw the giant Goliath. They figured the situation was hopeless. But optimistic David with his slingshot and stones thought, "He's so huge a target, how can I miss?"

One in four people is born with a brain that is hardwired for thinking positively about himself and his life. We call those lucky folks "optimists." However, the rest of us can choose to build a better self-talk system. The concepts in this book will help you recognize you thoughts and whether to modify them. Optimists understand the broad benefits of positive thinking on mind, body, and spirit. They're set on accentuating the positive and eliminating negative in themselves and everyone else.

It's well documented that optimists live longer, are happier, more successful, and more popular than their pessimistic counterparts. A Mayo Clinic study found that pessimists have a 19 percent greater likelihood of premature death than optimists. Optimists are flexible and resilient in their relationships and jobs no matter what problems come up. Ever see one of those "Weebles wobble but they don't fall down" toys? No matter how hard you knock them, they pop back up. That's an optimist.

I hope you'll refuse to stay down when you fall, because you are going to fall. We all do—it's part of life. What optimists have figured out is that a bad day doesn't constitute a bad life. An unpleasant event is only temporary, and it even can teach us something about ourselves or an unskilled choice we have made. It's all about keeping negative events in perspective.

CHAPTER EIGHTEEN

EMBRACE
the Attitude of Gratitude

I.Q. COUNTS FOR ONLY about 20 percent of a person's ability to succeed; the rest depends on optimism and learned people skills. A landmark book, *Emotional Intelligence* by Daniel Goldman, explains why the smartest kid in your high school didn't wind up rich and famous, while the likeable kid you barely remember may be a CEO with a happy marriage and a slew of friends. The guy with a good disposition had a high EQ, or emotional intelligence quotient, which includes the capacity to look on the bright side.

Practicing gratefulness is a proven way to reinforce a positive outlook. It's retroactive optimism, because it looks back to generate positive feelings. Gratitude shifts your concentration away from what's not working to notice what's going right in your life. As well as setting your thoughts on an optimistic start for each brand-new day, how about closing your night with a good word? No matter what is going on in your life, you can always find something to be grateful for— even if it's only that things aren't worse!

What special blessing can you give thanks for today?

GRATITUDE IS . . .

. . . pausing to acknowledge and enjoy what we have
and letting it sink in.

A NOTE FROM NAOMI
*Larry and I enjoy concluding
each night with a ritual of
stating our favorite thing that
happened. It causes a "great
fullness" in our hearts. These
small, meaningful, everyday
moments give shape to my days.
Start looking into the corners of
your life with awareness and
appreciation.*

And whatever you do in word or deed,
do all in the name of the Lord Jesus,
giving thanks to God
the Father through Him.

COLOSSIANS 3:17

Remember the gospel song that says, "Count your blessings, name them one by one."

Last night Larry and I were both grateful for the same thing. Our grandchildren Elijah and Grace had come over to spend the night. At twilight we sat in the freshly mowed grass of our front yard and sang songs they'd learned at camp. Earlier in the day, I'd signed a contract to do a cable television series, but worldly success can't compare to the intimate joy of watching my grandchildren or relaxing with my husband. Whenever you and I pause to acknowledge and enjoy what we have, our spirits are uplifted and our immune systems are boosted. It's the way life's supposed to be lived.

CHAPTER NINETEEN

BUILD A
Strong Heart with Affirmations

AFFIRMATIONS KEEP US CONNECTED to our higher power. They give us a practical way to focus. They're a means for being intentional. They remind us that through the promises of our birthright as children of God, we deserve to achieve all our goals, and everything is just the way it's supposed to be. Because we can't have both fear and peace in the same thought, affirmations ward off confusing and negative messages from outside sources.

Affirmations also stimulate your subconscious mind as a practical way to speak the truth about your future in advance. They're like going to a mental gym: in order to stay in peak condition, you have to exercise and firm up your positive self-beliefs. If I go a few days without making my positive personal affirmations, I don't feel as sharp or strong, and my self-confidence gets flabby!

To affirm is to get straight about an idea. What self-concept do you wish to solidify?

AN AFFIRMATION IS . . .

. . . another way to change your negative self-talk. Affirmations are positive, proactive, present-tense statements that you make to yourself.

A NOTE FROM NAOMI

I tell myself: "Everything right now is just the way it's supposed to be. I won't take conflict or hurt personally. I'm worthy to attract good things."

WISDOM
from the Bible

*For You, LORD, have made
me glad through Your work;
I will triumph in the works
of Your hands. O LORD,
how great are Your works!
. . . Those who are planted
in the house of the LORD
Shall flourish in the courts of
our God. They shall still bear
fruit in old age; They shall be
fresh and flourishing,
To declare that the LORD is
upright; He is my rock.*

PSALM 92:4-5, 13-15

Thanksgiving has always been
my favorite holiday because it's about
gratefulness, family, friends, food,
and fun—my favorite things. When
I was struggling with hepatitis C,
I'd put my coat over my pajamas
and enter our empty church in the
middle of a weekday. I'd kneel at
the pulpit and beg God for
strength, courage, and wisdom to
deal with my trials. After my
recovery, Wy and Ash put together
a gratefulness family reunion at the
farm. It was our end-of-a-season-in-
hell benediction.

"Benediction" is a word that
means "good word," the utterance
of good wishes at the end of a divine
ceremony. Knowing how good we
have it helps nurture, comfort, and
cushion us when we get knocked
down. I'm always touched when I

see people on the evening news who've lost everything to some disaster, yet are still thankful just to be
alive.

I write down affirmations and tape them in
my daily planner so I'm constantly seeing them
throughout the day. I'll read them over whenever I'm
feeling a little weak in the self-confidence department.
Put affirmations in a prominent place like your
refrigerator door, desk, or kitchen cabinet. You can
also record them and pop them in the tape player in
your car. Try completing the following statements:

I'm good at…
I'm known for my…
I like my…
I'm thankful for…
I feel good about…
My life is filled with positive…
I've already survived…
I know I can achieve…

CHAPTER TWENTY

Mind Your Mind
to Mend Your Body

IT'S SO IMPORTANT to pray for the answer—not about the problem. Someone once requested, "Pray for me, I'm getting the flu." I alerted this person that it was a negative prediction. Instead, I suggested we pray proactively: "My body is strong and able to overcome any problem." Your body is listening and believes and manifests everything you say!

Your mind is in every cell in your body. This means that what goes on in your mind affects not only your success and peace, but your health as well. That's because there is far less separation between mind and body than the medical community previously imagined.

Positive thoughts and happy emotions actually can boost our immune system's functions, while negative thoughts can diminish it. One of the most amazing findings I discovered was that unresolved events or issues from our pasts have been encoded on a cellular level throughout our bodies. Now you see why it's so critical to identify and purge negative, toxic memories!

Can you consider some ways a negative feeling or belief about yourself is keeping your immune system depressed?

YOUR MIND IS . . .

. . . in every cell in your body. This means that what goes on in your mind affects not only the quality of every day of your life, but your health as well.

A NOTE FROM NAOMI

When you ignore unpleasant emotions and experiences and don't deal with them, your body is left to absorb and eventually express them. As soon as I uncovered this important information, I figured that if my body was listening to everything I was thinking and saying, I'd better begin "medicating" it with positive, life-affirming thoughts!

WISDOM
from the Bible

If any of you lacks wisdom,
let him ask of God,
who gives to all liberally
and without reproach,
and it will be given to him.

JAMES 1:5

The fight-or-flight response is useful for a real and present danger—such as a person pointing a gun at us. We become physically mobilized to fight or run. Our hearts beat faster, and the blood vessels in our extremities constrict to prepare our large muscles for combat. But we don't fight off armed gunmen all day. The stresses you and I experience are lower-grade but chronic: waiting in traffic, coping with crying children, dealing with computer crashes. Many of us live with our fight-or-flight reaction on all the time. While stressing our minds, it also causes great wear and tear on our bodies. Immune system function goes down when the fight-or-flight system kicks in and stays turned on. It's meant to give us a temporary boost, not be on all the time. What this means is that the more we feel we are in danger, setting off the fight-or-flight response, the more danger we put ourselves in as we strain our immune system and heart.

A UCLA study involved having actors perform our negative states—like anger, shock, and sadness—and our positive states, such as joy, love, and gratitude. The effects of these emotions on the actors' bodily functions were measured. The results of either a happy or sad state were fairly short in duration—twenty to thirty minutes. States of sadness and happiness had different effects on certain immune processes. Both states produced some increase in the activity of natural killer cells that help the body fight infection, cancer, and the like. But the positive effects of laughter, trust, cuddling, and expressing good feelings actually improved immune functions. Your body believes you even when you're acting! Faith it till you make it!

The Mind, Spirit, Body
CONNECTION

MY CHILD, pay attention to my words;

listen closely to what I say.

Don't ever forget my words;

keep them always in mind.

They are the key to life for those who find them;

they bring health to the whole body.

Be careful what you think,

because your thoughts run your life.

PROVERBS 4:20-23 NCV

As a tree gives fruit, healing words give life,

but dishonest words crush the spirit.

PROVERBS 15:4 NCV

A happy heart is like good medicine,
but a broken spirit drains your strength.

PROVERBS 17:22

Jesus said to him,
"Then see. You are healed
because you believed."

LUKE 18:42 NCV

CHAPTER TWENTY-ONE

DON'T LET
Your Tongue Cut Your Throat

WHEN YOU ANGRILY CONFRONT someone, do you lash out? This only prompts other people to instantly become defensive. They get their hackles up and dig in their heels. Because the best defense is a good offense, they immediately begin coming up with ways to refute whatever you're saying. They're certainly not listening to you! They're busy either preparing to strike back at you or shouting over you. It's unlikely either of you will get through to the other one, let alone remember what was said. Don't try to match wits. It certainly may be appropriate to display your anger. But you must figure out how to do it in a constructive way where you stay in control of yourself.

Do you demand that it's "my way or the highway" when you argue? You may risk not seeing a family member or friend again.

PRONOUN THERAPY IS . . .

. . . changing your pronoun from "you" to "I" to allow you to effectively communicate anger by owning your feelings. The other person sees how a situation is affecting you. It's less of an attack on them and moves you closer to a resolution. So instead of "You make me so mad," choose "I'm mad."

A NOTE FROM NAOMI

Avoid using words like "always" and "never." They make it harder for the other person to agree or change. Interrupting, lecturing, or explaining the other person's behavior is also a definite argument loser. Don't forget—in any and every situation, you first must grasp your own feelings and change yourself before trying to change someone else. ✎

So then,

my beloved brethren,

let every man

be swift to hear,

slow to speak,

slow to wrath.

JAMES 1:19

No one can push our buttons better than our own families! They even installed them! They know all our stuff, so we are most vulnerable to them. F. Scott Fitzgerald thought so. He said: "Family quarrels are bitter things. They don't go according to any rules. They're not like aches or wounds; they're more like splits in the skin that won't heal because there's not enough material."

It's taken many years of hurt feelings, tantrums, and unresolved conflicts for my family to get to where we are now. I'd say our family now represents "enlightened imperfection." The room for improvement will always be the biggest room at the Judd house. Everyone got together at the kitchen table one night after supper and came up with guidelines for communicating difficult things. Here's what we all agreed on:

1. No interrupting.
2. No shouting.
3. Everyone must realize we all have our own reality.
4. Everyone gets as much time as they need to fully express themselves.
5. Everyone should be prepared with their thoughts and solutions so time isn't wasted.
6. Pause to think before you speak so you address the person as a friend.
7. No fair bringing others' opinions into it.
8. Silence can be another form of arguing. Say what's on your mind.
9. Everyone needs to be aware that there will always be some "issue."

CHAPTER TWENTY-TWO

PUT A STOP
to Worry and Fear

I FEARED SOMETHING was really wrong. I'd felt crummy off and on for two years. The periods of flu-like symptoms were becoming more intense and lasting longer. Then came that moment in the doctor's office when he proclaimed that I had hepatitis C.

Fear is pain about the future. The panic-producing prognosis of less than three years to live meant I had no future. What time I had would be miserable. I had come to believe that our mind is in every cell of our body. I knew I had to confront my fear, then learn how to control it. I couldn't allow myself to indulge in anxiety, because I knew my body could turn the doctor's prognosis into a self-fulfilling prophecy.

I also was constantly worried. Worry is pain about the present. Worry is like sitting in a rocking chair. It gives you something to do, but doesn't get you anywhere. Worry and fear occupy different temporal locations in our brains. Worry is more of a generalized, free-floating anxiety. It's the most common form of mental stress. We need to check out whether our anxieties are based on something real or whether our imagination is running away with us.

From the morning paper to the evening news, the media makes us anxious. Have you ever come in from a good day, turned on the news, and felt your mood darkening? TV can allow fear into your home, which should be your sanctuary. Be discerning.

WORRY IS . .

. . . pain about the present. Fear is pain about the future.

> ## A NOTE FROM NAOMI
> *I call upon my guardian angels when I'm worried.*
> *As a child playing on my grandparents' farm,*
> *I had an imaginary friend I considered my*
> *guardian angel. Her name was Elizabeth.*
> *Now I realize I have many angels, as I've found*
> *more than three hundred scriptures about them.*
> *When I find myself caught up in some worry,*
> *I envision these divine, protective, angelic*
> *archetypes standing guard all around me.* ✎

For God has not given us

a spirit of fear,

but of power and of love

and of a sound mind.

2 TIMOTHY 1:7

Fear is the darkroom where our negatives develop! The acronym FEAR stands for "**F**alse **E**vidence **A**ppearing **R**eal." If you don't identify and release your fear, it will leave you powerless and unable to stand up for yourself. An unresolved fear also can develop into an illness and then go on to prevent you from recuperating. Fear is the greatest inhibitor of the human spirit. Fear thrives on a lack of self-confidence and prevents us from taking risks.

Worry never gets you anywhere. A quiet, calm mind clears the way for constructive planning. Doing all you can by planning, calm breathing, using specific mood words, calling your angels, and remembering to be in God's presence are all proactive moves that help you live contentedly in the moment. Be sure to reward yourself when you do master your worry and keep on stamping out the worry bug.

CHAPTER TWENTY-THREE

TAKE A DAILY
Quiet Rest Time with God

ONE EFFECTIVE WAY to eliminate worry and fear over the long term is to meditate. Meditation creates a sense of self-mastery, inner stillness, and stability. Research even shows that meditation actually changes your mind's inclination to feel negative emotions like fear and worry, replacing it with the tendency to feel positive emotions like hope, optimism, and gratitude.

Meditation also strengthens your inner witness, the deeper part of yourself that becomes more and more aware of the movement of your thoughts. With a strong inner witness, you are aware of your worries without getting overly involved with them. "Oh, there I go getting afraid about money again." You begin to notice that while such thoughts do arise, they also disappear.

Are you ready to accept responsibility for your thoughts and commit to some quiet time each day?

MEDITATION IS . . .

. . . a quiet time when you get in touch with your inner witness. You can focus on a Bible verse, mental image of Jesus, or a visual representation of an inspiring thought, such as a white bird's feather to represent peace or the Holy Spirit.

A NOTE FROM NAOMI

When you start to picture something going wrong, remember you're in charge of telling your mind what to think. You can direct and produce all the scenes going on in your brain. You can rehearse the same scene but work out a happy ending to it. Focus on a positive outcome. If you drift to a negative, refocus on good so you can close your eyes and tell yourself, "I'm the director in this story. I can change this right now."

Be merciful to me, O God,
  be merciful to me!
  For my soul trusts in You;
And in the shadow of Your wings
  I will make my refuge,
  Until these calamities have passed by.
I will cry out to God Most High,
  To God who performs all things for me.
He shall send from heaven and save me;
  He reproaches the one
  who would swallow me up.

    SELAH

  God shall send forth
    His mercy and His truth.

PSALM 57:1-3

You begin to practice your faith when you take responsibility for your thoughts. I realize that everything happens for a reason—as part of a larger plan to grow in love and wisdom and be of service—and this helps me realize not to take problems personally. I trust in a divine intelligence that helps me relax in my life. When fear knocks at the door, faith answers, no one is there!

Make your home a sanctuary, a psychological fortress. Be sure it's comfy, calm, and pleasing so it can be your heart's resting place. Decorate with objects that give you fond memories of who you are. They will help you keep centered and stable.

Remember, there are always going to be things to cause fear or worry. But you and I get to decide which ones are real threats. Then we can choose how to handle them. Will you join me in choosing peace and happiness from now on?

CHAPTER TWENTY-FOUR

RESIGN AS
General Manager of the Universe

CHALLENGES ACTUALLY CAN be blessings because they allow us to take stock of our lives. One beneficial thing hepatitis C did for me was that it made me face up to my perfectionism. While I was ill, I didn't have the energy to indulge my usual perfectionistic ways. Instead, I sat in bed watching my husband fold the laundry the "wrong" way. My mother was putting pots in the "wrong" kitchen cabinet. Ashley was home from college leaving behind a messy trail throughout the house. Suddenly, Wynonna blew in with a new puppy to cheer me up. It immediately peed on my bed. I was thrown into a perfectionist spasm. Larry, Mom, Ash, and Wy gathered around on the bed, laughing merrily and playing with the puppy. At that moment I had a breakthrough instead of a breakdown. I decided to do some emotional housecleaning and resign as general manager of the universe. I could no longer be my old do-it-all self. It wasn't an option— I just didn't have the strength. Besides, it was standing in the way of having more fun and pleasure.

Are you a perfectionist?

PERFECTIONISM IS . . .

. . . when we play "What's wrong with this picture?" with life! We don't pay attention to what's right about the picture; we're just focused on finding fault. We're standing outside of life nitpicking at little things, finding fault, and then judging. Meantime, we're not fully participating in or occupying our lives, let alone enjoying ourselves.

> ### A NOTE FROM NAOMI
> *Kelsey Grammer once had me do a call-in for his popular show,* Frasier, *in which he played a radio show psychologist. I was playing an uptight perfectionist. Frasier's advice to my character was: "Next time your perfectionist tendencies hinder you, remember this quotation from Henry James: 'Excellence does not require perfection.' "*

Now a certain ruler asked [Jesus], saying,
"Good Teacher, what shall I do to inherit eternal life?"
So Jesus said to him, "Why do you call Me good?
No one is good but One, that is, God.
You know the commandments:
'Do not commit adultery,'
'Do not murder,' 'Do not steal,'
'Do not bear false witness,'
'Honor your father and your mother.'"

And he said, "All these things I have kept from my youth."

So when Jesus heard these things,
He said to him, "You still lack one thing.
Sell all that you have and distribute to the poor,
and you will have treasure in heaven;
and come, follow Me."

LUKE 18:18-22

While it's important to strive for personal excellence, we never can be perfect. You and I are already enough. In fact, it is our imperfections that make us unique and real. A Navajo rug weaver in Sedona, Arizona, once told me the Navajo wisdom on this subject. She pointed out a purposeful flaw in her rug: "We believe if we attain perfection, our life is over."

You and I can't pay attention to the picture of our lives if we are too busy dusting the frame! My eyes opened to how lucky I was to have a close, loving family around me who cared so much. The hum of our household's daily activity, the sound of familiar laughter, and the playful noises of an adorable puppy were the beautiful music and rhythm of my life. I decided to start dancing to it. Care to join me?

The rewards were immediate. It was a relief to not always have to lead. Others were just as capable, and it was time for those who weren't to begin to learn. My girls began to see the bigger picture themselves. They recognized me as a vulnerable human being instead of Supermom. My family enjoyed feeling needed, and our interdependence drew us even closer.

CHAPTER TWENTY-FIVE

LOOK INTO
the Mirror of Truth

TAKE A LOOK into the Mirror of Truth here: on a scale of one to ten, how much of a people-pleaser are you? When you're resenting an obligation or a person, stare at yourself in the mirror and ask, "What is my motivation here?" As you penetrate below excuses and rationales, you'll see the answer most likely lies in a poor sense of self-worth. Why on earth would you feel that you're not good enough just being yourself?

What I discovered when I turned in my pink slip on running the world is that you and I have to be willing to disappoint somebody else in order to be true to ourselves. Now I use phrases like "I can't, but I'll show you how," and even just plain "No." It's a terrific word/sentence! "No" is now my word of choice whenever I'm feeling pressure, obligation, or resentment.

PERSONAL QUESTION

Why on earth would you feel you should do something to please someone else because you're not good enough just being yourself?

TO DELEGATE IS . . .

Rather than do something that I either don't have the time or energy for, I appoint and oversee competent others to do it.

A NOTE FROM NAOMI

When we fall for the notion that we need to be in charge of everything, we're not standing up for ourselves. It harms our relationships, self-esteem, and even health, because stress from doing too much increases the deleterious hormones cortisol and catecholamine norepinephrine.

WISDOM
from the Bible

The poet Robert Frost was right: "Good fences make good neighbors." Good emotional boundaries help us understand where we end and others begin. Each of us has an invisible territorial perimeter, usually about three feet in American culture. Doesn't it make you uncomfortable when someone, especially a stranger, stands too close? Obviously, if someone shoves us or touches us suggestively, they're trespassing.

Emotional boundaries are every bit as necessary to define and protect our individuality and character. Until we decide what ours are, we'll be unclear what we're responsible for and what we aren't.

Too many women don't understand the importance of setting healthy boundaries. In any relationship, it's critical that women have good physical, emotional, and sexual boundaries. Mothers who are people-pleasers send bad signals of unworthiness to their kids. Teenage girls aren't taught self-esteem and how to say "No." Instead, they are taught to put other people's feelings first, and that spells trouble as they begin to date. Small children need to bond and identify with their caregivers as they're growing, but they need to begin disengaging as they reach their teens. By adulthood, they should have a firm sense of where they end and others begin.

No matter what age, you must establish boundaries. As you learn more about what you like and don't like, you can better explain it to others. Establishing emotional boundaries allows you to prevent your self-respect and character from being intruded upon.

CHAPTER TWENTY-SIX

Have Purpose
with a Passion

YOU WON'T FIND YOUR PURPOSE by asking for directions from the guy at the gas station. Purpose is found when each of us comes to understand our gifts and passions. It's what deeply matters to you.

Each and every one of us wants to know that our life matters, that there is a reason for our existence. One of my psychologist friends has an outgoing phone message saying, "Tell me who you are and what you want." If you pause to consider these questions in metaphysical terms, they are the ultimate, thought-provoking questions. These questions can't be easily answered. They only can be explored and learned from as we constantly ask them over and over.

PERSONAL QUESTIONS

Where do you want to make a difference?

Where do you want to aim your talents?

What kind of suffering upsets you?

A PERSONAL MISSION STATEMENT IS . . .

. . . a statement that identifies your priorities and points you in the direction you wish to go. It's your own commitment to yourself regarding what you desire to be doing. Your personal mission statement can help you decide what to add to your daily activities so that you come closer to fulfilling your mission

A NOTE FROM NAOMI

Here's what I came up with: "My mission is to slow down, simplify, and be kind so that I can help alleviate suffering and promote happiness in other people—particularly women—through self-awareness." In order for me to create this statement, it was crucial for me to know my values—what I want and what really matters to me. ✎

We brought nothing into this world, and it is certain we can carry nothing out. And having food and clothing, with these we shall be content. But those who desire to be rich fall into temptation and a snare, and into many foolish and harmful lusts which drown men.

1 TIMOTHY 6:7-9

Voluntary simplicity is not depriving. It's the exact opposite. I like to be "free to be." Success isn't stuff; it's relationships. It's enjoying what we have. I now plan my schedule very carefully. If I don't watch it my day is gone faster than the speed of life! I don't prioritize my schedule anymore; instead I just schedule my priorities.

As far as the rest of my mission statement—being kind and helping to alleviate suffering and promote happiness—well, that's partly what I am doing writing this book. I'm practicing my religion. I take the word "kindness" to mean "to treat like real kin." I want you to be happy and healthy enough to enjoy all the minutes in your day, every day.

More than 150 years ago Henry David Thoreau said, "Our life is frittered away by detail . . . Simplify, simplify, then simplify some more." This is even more relevant today! Are you living in a kingdom of stuff? Are your laborsaving devices freeing you up, or do you sometimes feel like a slave to them?

A girlfriend's grandmother came to visit at my friend's new home. Sitting in the kitchen surrounded by a variety of the latest appliances, she had to ask, "Grandma, if you could have only one modern convenience, which would you pick?" Grandmother answered thoughtfully, "Running water." Join me in getting back to basics so that you have time to enjoy every day and every night.

CHAPTER TWENTY-SEVEN

THE POWER
of Togetherness

YOU AND I DON'T do well alone. Studies have shown that women who feel isolated succumb to breast cancer and ovarian cancer at several times the normal, expected rate. College students who report cold relationships with parents have early onset of hypertension. Women with smaller social networks give birth to smaller babies. Heart attack survivors who live alone die at twice the rate of those who live with others. Got your attention?

When I first got sick, I lay alone in my darkened bedroom, and it began to occur to me that I'd always been the one to whom others came for help. Now I was indeed "the friend in need." I began circling the wagons and calling the cavalry. I summoned a prayer healing with the elders of our church. I surrendered my pride and allowed Wy and Ash to see I was vulnerable, which allowed them to feel needed. Larry became my prayer warrior.

It is essential that you create and maintain a good support system. Who is part of your support system? Whose support system are you a part of?

A TRUE FRIEND IS . . .

. . . one of the greatest supports we can have in our lives. Having a true friend is like sitting together on a swing for an hour, and not saying a word, and then coming away believing that it was the best conversation you ever had.

> ### A NOTE FROM NAOMI
> *Because I'm away from home so much and around people all the time, when I am at the farm I'm happy to stay put. I dig in like a flea on a hound. Larry complained that we hadn't developed enough couples relationships. So we consciously built our network of several couples. We gather under the big shade tree in our backyard on Saturday nights for what we call "The World According to Us" discussions.*

WISDOM
from the Bible

A friend loves at all times.

PROVERBS 17:17

Who's your oldest friend? Do you have friends of different ages? The love of friends is good for us—body, mind, and soul. When I'm with my friends from childhood, I'm stirred by feelings of love, appreciation, and understanding. We chastise one another when one of us is stuck in negative or irrational thinking. Because we have a long personal history, we can point out times when the other survived a crisis. We do constructive, supportive activities such as exercising and walking together. There's a group of older gals I know of who walk laps inside a mall regularly. They call themselves "The Brazen Hussies." Exercising with friends helps us stay with the workout. That's support for your mind, body, and soul.

As we get our acts together by figuring out what we want and discovering that we are lovable, we begin to attract people with healthier self-esteem and better boundaries. The more work I did on myself, the more high-quality people entered my support system. Along the way, I consciously sought out those who saw things in me that I was not aware of and who helped me grow. In other words, mentors.

But support comes in all shapes and sizes. If you're one of the 58 million cat owners or 53 million dog owners, you won't need statistics to prove the benefits of being a pet lover. My constant canine companion, Tilly, is in my lap as I write this. Behavioral scientists know for sure that people who care for pets recover faster from illness. Pets lift our spirits, help us be more optimistic, and give us a purpose through being responsible for them.

WE NEED EACH OTHER

At this time you have plenty.
What you have can help others who are in need.
Then later, when they have plenty,
they can help you when you are in need,
and all will be equal.

2 CORINTHIANS 8:14 NCV

MY CHILDREN, WE SHOULD LOVE PEOPLE
not only with words and talk,
but by our actions and true caring.

1 JOHN 3:18 NCV

Most importantly, love each other deeply,
because love will cause many sins to be forgiven.
Open your homes to each other, without complaining.
Each of you has received a gift to use to serve others.
Be good servants of God's various gifts of grace.

1 PETER 4:8-10 NCV

When we honestly ask ourselves which person in our lives means the most to us, we often find that it is those who, instead of giving advice, solutions, or cures, have chosen rather to share our pain and touch our wounds with a warm and tender hand.

HENRY NOUWEN

FRIENDS ARE AN
AID TO THE YOUNG,
TO GUARD THEM
FROM ERROR;
TO THE ELDERLY,
TO ATTEND TO THEIR
WANTS, AND TO
SUPPLEMENT THEIR
FAILING POWER OF
ACTION; TO THOSE IN
THE PRIME OF LIFE,
TO ASSIST THEM TO
NOBLE DEEDS.

ARISTOTLE

CHAPTER TWENTY-EIGHT

SURVIVORS
Practice Eight Things

I WANTED TO LIVE. So I set out seeking ways to survive my death sentence from hepatitis C. My crisis presented opportunity as well as danger as I chose the opportunity to explore new dimensions in medicine. My therapist presented psychological evidence that survivors of difficulties—whether emotional, physical, or circumstantial—all seem to display eight specific characteristics. They are:

1. Strong Spiritual Belief
2. Strong Support System
3. Sense of Humor
4. Connection to Nature
5. Goals
6. Good Nutrition
7. Regular Exercise and Rest
8. Openness to New Experiences

Which of the eight characteristics of a survivor personality do you already have? Which have you not yet considered?

COMPLEMENTARY HEALING METHODS MEANS...

What we Americans call "complementary" methods of healing really are standard practice in 80 percent of the world. Healing touch, scented oils, and prayer are written about in the Bible, although it may be a new experience for "modern" culture to consider.

A NOTE FROM NAOMI

Working as an R.N., I often witnessed subtle ways my patients were healing that weren't medically induced. I knew there were forces at work I couldn't explain. You can't beat modern medicine for surgical intervention, emergency trauma care, screening and testing, or antibiotics. But there are many other effective healing methods we can use for ourselves that are less intrusive, less invasive, and less costly.

WISDOM
from the Bible

Is anyone among you sick? Let him call for the elders of the church, and let them pray over him, anointing him with oil in the name of the Lord. And the prayer of faith will save the sick, and Lord will raise him up. And if he has committed sins, he will be forgiven.

JAMES 5:14-15

Many patients unfortunately still see their doctors as deities in lab coats whose omniscient hands hold their outcome. Survivors, however, see their doctors as partners on their journey to wellness, so they are discerning in selecting Dr. Right. They care how much a doctor knows but are just as concerned about how much he or she cares. These patients accept that they must be in charge of investigating every avenue toward their own healing.

I've come to realize the benefits of complementary techniques. My dear friend the Reverend Robert Schuller even had me on his worldwide TV program, *The Hour of Power,* to substantiate the scriptural authority behind adding these complementary measures.

I have referred to prayer many times because I am living proof of its healing power. Spiritual isolation results in stress.

There is ample evidence that, in the words of Harvard cardiologist Herbert Benson, "we may be wired for God." Prayer reminds me that I belong to God and am part of the universe. Prayer not only can change things, it did change me. When I was sick, I had a healing prayer service at my church in which the elders laid their hands on me, anointed me with oils, and prayed for my healing.

I never use the term "alternate medicine" for fear of implying that it's a matter of choosing between these approaches and mainstream medicine. I can testify that using both together is better. I was monitoring my liver function, getting a biopsy, and taking the drug interferon. But every night, as I drew up the interferon into the syringe, I knelt at my own altar and incorporated complementary techniques. I prayed while injecting the medicine.

CHAPTER TWENTY-NINE

LOVE IS
the Greatest Healer

THE JUDDS HAVE ALWAYS BEEN about audience participation, but during our 1991 Farewell Tour many of the fans lining up around the bus were dealing with all manner of illnesses and crises. They had heard about my hepatitis C and came to be inspired by our music, get insights into how we were handling our crises, and share their own stories. The first such fan to approach us was a mother with several children. She'd just had a radical mastectomy. Her husband, unable to deal with her illness, had deserted her. As we listened tearfully to her plight, she and I began supporting each other. This was the first time I'd ever prayed with a stranger. Something marvelous was happening. As I shared stories with more people, I saw how much we had in common. We chose to become better instead of bitter, and both sides experienced breakthroughs. Wy began calling me a "musicianary."

Dr. Blair Justice, author of *Who Gets Sick: How Beliefs, Moods, and Thoughts Affect Your Health*, visited the bus after one performance and teased, "I know exactly what you are doing out there, missy. You're absorbing the energy from those thousands of supportive fans and your passion for music and communicating to boost your body's beleaguered immune system." Busted!

PERSONAL QUESTION

Are you comfortable praying with others? I wasn't.

But Wynonna reminded me, "God doesn't call the qualified, He qualifies the called."

HELPER'S HIGH IS . . .

. . . a kind of euphoria volunteers get when helping others—a warm glow in the chest and a sense of calm. It is comparable to a runner's high, and is caused by the body's release of our favorite neurochemicals, endorphins.

A NOTE FROM NAOMI

If you are looking for a way to be of service to others, there's no easier place to start than by being a good listener. Do you listen with your heart as well as your ears? You'll impress someone much more with attentive silence than you can by trying to top their stories.

Jesus said, "A new command I give you:
Love one another.
As I have loved you,
so you must love one another.
By this all men will know that
you are my disciples,
if you love one another."

JOHN 13:34-35

Service is the work of the soul. It pays spiritual and psychological dividends. You feel engaged with the rest of humanity. You're taking a step toward solving some problem. You're making things better, which serves you and others well. When you reach out to others in distress, you see your own blessings more clearly. You become aware of what you've been taking for granted and what you're glad you don't have.

Research supports this notion that when we give to others, we give mental, emotional, spiritual, and physical health to ourselves. Michigan researchers who studied twenty-seven hundred people for almost ten years found that men who regularly did volunteer work had death rates two-and-one-half times lower than men who didn't. Perhaps this is why some of our nation's most generous philanthropists, like John D. Rockefeller (age ninety-eight), have lived to such ripe old ages.

Every one of us has the capacity to affect the healing of others. When we act in loving ways toward others, we are strengthening not only our own immune systems, but those of the people we help. A win-win situation.

CHAPTER THIRTY

LIVE IN
God's Presence and Stay in the Light

ALL THAT HAPPENS TO US, good and bad, presents great possibilities for emotional and spiritual growth. You and I have free will. We can pick and choose what better serves our happiness. I hope the concepts in this book are helping you gain clarity about what behaviors you want to release. My wish is that you come to understand what's no longer serving you well. I'm living proof that all of our difficulties can be steppingstones to self-actualization and fulfillment. But I'm just a messenger. Are you willing to open your eyes to see the choices that will turn your scars into stars?

Ultimately any chance for personal happiness comes down to realizing that This Is It. This is your one and only short and precious life. It could end at any time. This present moment is really all the time we have to decide to follow God and live in His light. I hope this book has informed. God's word transforms.

PERSONAL QUESTION

This is just the beginning . . . where do you want to grow from here?

THE WORD 'PROMISE' . . .

. . . comes from the Latin word that means "to send forth." My books and music are a promise I made to help those who asked for a look inside my struggles in order to deal with their own crises. Your life can be full of promise as you are sent forth to help others as well.

A NOTE FROM NAOMI

Now these are my parting words to you as you come to the end of this book. This is really your beginning. The more you come to understand the transformative power of these breakthrough choices, the more you will know peace.

WISDOM
from the Bible

Jesus said, "Peace I leave with you. My peace I give to you; not as the world gives do I give to you. Let not your heart be troubled, neither let it be afraid."

JOHN 14:27

I was rushing to catch a plane one day, and a gentleman hurried over. I could see he was very ill. With tear-filled eyes, he began to tell me that he'd been following my journey. He was now headed home to break the news to his family that he was dying of AIDS. He'd sent them our CD with a song I wrote, "Love Can Build a Bridge," along with a letter preparing them for his arrival. As the gate agents called us, he pleaded, "What can you tell me?"

It all seemed preposterous: a stranger preparing to make life's final passage was seeking words of wisdom from me. In such instances, I've learned to live in the present and in God's presence. I chose to stand still and let God move.

The word "peace" tumbled out. "Peace assures you that you are loved and never alone—that everything is all right just the way it is. Fear is robbing you of enjoying your moments. It is not how many breaths you take in your lifetime that matters; it's how many moments that take your breath away. You can choose peace with every breath. Join our circle of believers who choose to walk toward the light. Take comfort in the revelation that peace of mind is the ultimate goal for all of us. All is well. All is well."

Henri Nouwen wrote, "In the giving it becomes clear that we are chosen, blessed, and broken not simply for our own sakes, but so that all we are about, all that we live, finds its final significance in its being lived for others."

GOD'S PROMISE OF PEACE

I will give peace,
REAL PEACE,
to those far and near, and I will heal them,"
says the LORD.   ISAIAH 57:19 NCV

> *"I leave you peace; my peace*
> *I give you. I do not give it to you*
> *as the world does. So don't let your*
> *hearts be troubled or afraid. . . .*
> *I told you these things so that you can*
> *have peace in me.*
> *In this world you will have trouble,*
> *but be brave!*
> *I have defeated the world."*
>
> JOHN 14:27, 33 NCV

Do not worry about anything, but pray and ask God
for everything you need, always giving thanks.
And God's peace, which is so great we cannot understand it,
will keep your hearts and minds in Christ Jesus.

PHILIPPIANS 4:6-7 NCV

PEACE IS THE GIFT OF GOD.

Do you want peace?

Go to God.

Do you want peace in your families?

Go to God.

Do you want peace to brood over your families?

If you do, live your religion, and the very peace

of God will dwell and abide with you,

for that is where peace comes from,

and it doesn't dwell anywhere else.

JOHN TAYLOR

NAOMI JUDD

www.naomijudd.com

"I'm a communicator" says Naomi Judd, "whether I'm expressing myself through writing a song or a book or I am singing, acting, speaking at an engagement or even chatting one-on-one with a stranger on the street. Finding a way to share common experiences is my grand passion."

Naomi first expressed this passion of communication as half of country music's most famous mother/daughter team, The Judds. Their popularity earned them twenty top 10 hits (including fifteen number 1's) and kept them undefeated for eight consecutive years at all three major country music awards shows. In addition, the duo won five Grammys and a vast array of other awards and honors. As a songwriter, Naomi also won a Grammy for "Country Song of the Year" with the Judds' international hit "Love Can Build A Bridge."

In 1991, after selling more than 20 million albums and videos in a mere seven years and at the pinnacle of their phenomenal career, The Judds' reign came to an abrupt end. Naomi was diagnosed with Hepatitis C, a potentially fatal chronic liver disease that forced her retirement. Their "Farewell" tour was the top grossing tour and their farewell concert was the most successful musical event in cable pay-per-view history.

With unwavering optimism and characteristic inner strength, Naomi stepped out of the spotlight to explore paths that have led to new successful endeavors. Today, she is completely cured of the Hepatitis C virus and uses the strength of her own experiences as spokesperson for the American Liver Foundation. In 1991, Naomi created the Naomi Judd Education and Research Fund, using her household name and personal time to raise invaluable awareness of the deadly Hepatitis C virus as well as research funds for the American Liver Foundation. For more information, see www.naomijudd.com.

Though her creativity continues to flow through music and writing, today Naomi also expresses her energy on humanitarian activities, social issues and personal growth education. Her natural ability to act as a translator between academic communities and everyday people makes her a truly unique figure.

Naomi also combines her passion for communicating and her love of children in *Gertie the Goldfish and the Christmas Surprise,* a new book about family, love, true gifts— and a very special surprise.

Former registered nurse. Well-versed in women's health concerns, she sings the benefits of harmony between mind, body and spirit.

Former uninsured single mom on welfare. Naomi advocates health care reform on behalf of the 44 million Americans who have no medical coverage.

Former domestic violence victim. Naomi's dramatic story as a victim of domestic violence makes her a powerful speaker against such injustices. She shows how emotional and physical scars can be transformed into inner strength and fulfillment.

Mother of two highly successful daughters. One of Naomi's priorities is the restoration of the family. Daughters Ashley and Wynonna, along with their husbands and children, share adjoining farms with Naomi, making it convenient for their "family time" activities and "get togethers."

Humanitarian. Believing that "service is the work of the soul and we're here to grow in love, wisdom and be of service," Naomi is active in numerous humanitarian and social issues.

Entrepreneur. Her best-selling skin care line, "Esteem", combines the best of skin science and Naomi's philosophy on the importance of self esteem.

Teacher. In addition to her writing, she has a new TV show called *Naomi's New Morning* on the Hallmark Channel.

This is my prayer for you:

that your love will grow more and more;

that you will have knowledge

and understanding with your love;

that you will see the difference

between good and bad and will choose the good;

that you will be pure

and without wrong for the coming of Christ;

that you will do many good things

with the help of Christ

to bring glory and praise to God.

PHILIPPIANS 1:9-11 NCV